Green Bay Packers

BY
ZACH WYNER

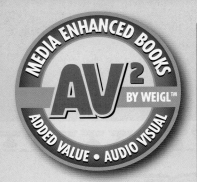

AV² provides enriched content that supplements and complements this book. Weigl's AV² books strive to create inspired learning and engage young minds in a total learning experience.

Your AV² Media Enhanced books come alive with...

Audio
Listen to sections of the book read aloud.

Key Words
Study vocabulary, and complete a matching word activity.

Video
Watch informative video clips.

Quizzes
Test your knowledge.

Embedded Weblinks
Gain additional information for research.

Slide Show
View images and captions, and prepare a presentation.

Try This!
Complete activities and hands-on experiments.

... and much, much more!

Go to **www.av2books.com**, and enter this book's unique code.

BOOK CODE

N 1 6 1 9 4 2

AV² by Weigl brings you media enhanced books that support active learning.

Published by AV² by Weigl
350 5th Avenue, 59th Floor
New York, NY 10118
Websites: www.av2books.com   www.weigl.com

Library of Congress Control Number: 2014930847

ISBN 978-1-4896-0826-0 (hardcover)
ISBN 978-1-4896-0828-4 (single-user eBook)
ISBN 978-1-4896-0829-1 (multi-user eBook)

Printed in the United States of America in North Mankato, Minnesota
1 2 3 4 5 6 7 8 9 0 18 17 16 15 14

042014
WEP150314

Project Coordinator Aaron Carr
Art Director Terry Paulhus

Photo Credits
Every reasonable effort has been made to trace ownership and to obtain permission to reprint copyright material. The publishers would be pleased to have any errors or omissions brought to their attention so that they may be corrected in subsequent printings.

Weigl acknowledges Getty Images as its primary image supplier for this title.

Green Bay Packers

CONTENTS

When considering how important the Green Bay Packers are to the sport of professional football, consider these facts: the Green Bay Packers have won an impressive 13 National Football League (NFL) Championships, including two **Super Bowl** titles. This record number is more than any other team in NFL history. Also, 22 Packers have been inducted in the Pro Football **Hall of Fame**, and the NFL Championship trophy is named after Packers' Hall of Fame coach Vince Lombardi.

The Green Bay Packers are not only a symbol of excellence, they are also a symbol of passion, integrity, and dedication. From the "Cheesehead" fan to the **most valuable player (MVP)** quarterback Aaron Rodgers, every human being involved with the Packers' organization lives and breathes football, and they do it in a way that commands respect.

Green Bay, Wisconsin is the smallest professional sports town in North America.

The passion of their fans comes as no surprise. The people of Green Bay, Wisconsin, quite literally own their beloved Packers. The Green Bay Packers are the only non-profit, community-owned major league professional sports team in the United States.

Aaron Rodgers is the current starting quarterback for the Packers. He was drafted by Green Bay in 2005.

Stadium Lambeau Field

Division National Football Conference (NFC) North

Head coach Mike McCarthy

Location Green Bay, Wisconsin

NFL championships 1929, 1930, 1931, 1936, 1939, 1944, 1961, 1962, 1965, 1966, 1967, 1996, 2010

Nicknames The Green and Gold, The Pack, The Big Bay Blues, Acme Packers, Bays, Blues

29
Playoff Appearances

13
NFL Championships

15
Division Championships

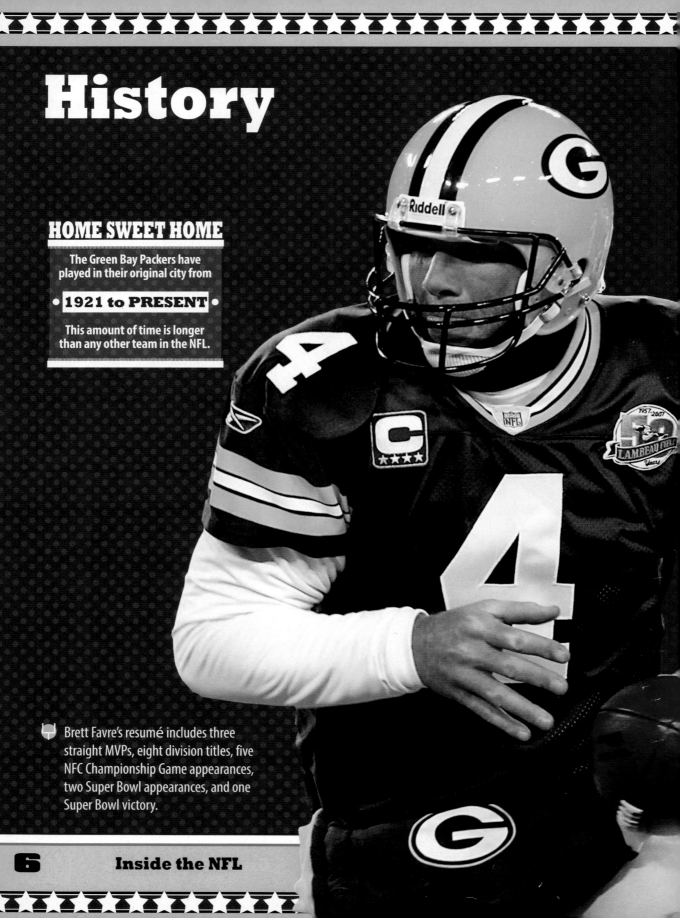

History

HOME SWEET HOME

The Green Bay Packers have played in their original city from

• 1921 to PRESENT •

This amount of time is longer than any other team in the NFL.

Brett Favre's resumé includes three straight MVPs, eight division titles, five NFC Championship Game appearances, two Super Bowl appearances, and one Super Bowl victory.

Founded in 1919 by Curly Lambeau and George Whitney Calhoun, the Green Bay Packers are the third-oldest NFL franchise. In 1923, the Green Bay Football Corporation was founded, ensuring that the Packers would be a publicly owned franchise. Many people credit public ownership as the reason the Packers have remained in the small city of Green Bay all these years. A winner of six NFL titles in 29 years, Curly Lambeau stepped down as the Packers head coach in 1950. It took a little more than a decade, but the Packers returned to the top of the sport behind hall of fame coach Vince Lombardi. From 1959 to 1967, Lombardi led numerous future hall of famers to five championships while losing only one **postseason** game.

In 1993, a long drought that had seen the Packers qualify for the **playoffs** just twice in 25 years came to a close with the blossoming of quarterback Brett Favre. Over the next 14 seasons, Favre would lead the Pack to 11 playoff appearances and a Super Bowl title. Following Favre's retirement, Cheeseheads did not have to wait long to return to the Super Bowl. After joining the Packers in the 2005 **NFL Draft**, Aaron Rodgers soon become an NFL MVP and a Super Bowl champion.

Widely projected as the first pick in the 2005 NFL Draft, Aaron Rodgers slipped to 24th overall and landed in Green Bay.

Green Bay Packers

The Stadium

Lambeau Field is named for former Packers head coach Curly Lambeau.

Lambeau Field is the second oldest stadium in the NFL behind Chicago's Soldier Field. It has housed the Packers for an NFL-record 57 years. Opened in 1957, Lambeau underwent major renovations in the early 2000s. Today, it can comfortably seat 80,750 screaming Packers fans.

Of course, while their seats may be comfortable, the same cannot always be said of the weather. With an average temperature of 43.8 °Fahrenheit (6.6 °Celsius), Lambeau Field is the coldest stadium in the NFL. The 1967 NFL Championship Game in Green Bay is known today as the "Ice Bowl." Following that game, the Kentucky bluegrass playing field at Lambeau earned the nickname "Frozen Tundra." That day, temperatures dipped well below freezing, as the Packers beat the New York Giants, 21-17.

Every Packers home game has sold out since 1960.

While taking in a game at Lambeau Field, cold fans warm their bellies with a bowl of Booyah soup and a side of cheese curds.

Where They Play

CANADA

Lake Superior

30 Washington

Oregon

Montana

North Dakota

Minnesota

23 Wisconsin

22

Idaho

South Dakota

24

29

Nevada

Wyoming

14

Nebraska

Iowa

13 Illinois

15

Utah

Colorado

Kansas

Missouri

California

UNITED STATES

31

16

Arizona

New Mexico

Oklahoma

Arkansas

32

Pacific Ocean

17

Texas

Mississippi

Louisiana

12

27

Alaska

0   500 Miles
0   500 km

Hawai'i

0   100 Miles
0   100 km

MEXICO

Gulf of Mexico

AMERICAN FOOTBALL CONFERENCE

EAST		NORTH		SOUTH		WEST	
1	Gillette Stadium	5	FirstEnergy Stadium	9	EverBank Field	13	Arrowhead Stadium
2	MetLife Stadium	6	Heinz Field	10	LP Field	14	Sports Authority Field at Mile High
3	Ralph Wilson Stadium	7	M&T Bank Stadium	11	Lucas Oil Stadium	15	O.co Coliseum
4	Sun Life Stadium	8	Paul Brown Stadium	12	NRG Stadium	16	Qualcomm Stadium

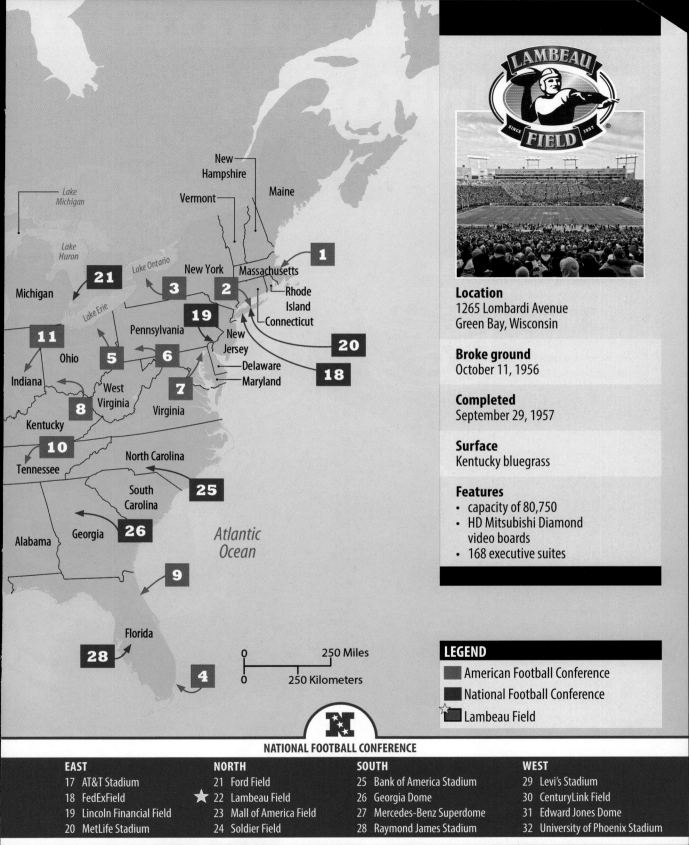

Lake Michigan

Lake Huron

Lake Ontario

Lake Erie

New Hampshire

Vermont

Maine

Michigan

21

3

New York

Massachusetts

2

1

Rhode Island

Connecticut

19

Ohio

11

5

6

Pennsylvania

New Jersey

20

18

Indiana

8

7

Delaware

Maryland

West Virginia

Virginia

Kentucky

10

Tennessee

North Carolina

South Carolina

25

Alabama

Georgia

26

Atlantic Ocean

9

Florida

28

4

| 0 | | 250 Miles |
| 0 | | 250 Kilometers |

Location
1265 Lombardi Avenue
Green Bay, Wisconsin

Broke ground
October 11, 1956

Completed
September 29, 1957

Surface
Kentucky bluegrass

Features
- capacity of 80,750
- HD Mitsubishi Diamond video boards
- 168 executive suites

LEGEND
■ American Football Conference
■ National Football Conference
☆ Lambeau Field

NATIONAL FOOTBALL CONFERENCE

EAST	NORTH	SOUTH	WEST
17 AT&T Stadium	21 Ford Field	25 Bank of America Stadium	29 Levi's Stadium
18 FedExField	☆ 22 Lambeau Field	26 Georgia Dome	30 CenturyLink Field
19 Lincoln Financial Field	23 Mall of America Field	27 Mercedes-Benz Superdome	31 Edward Jones Dome
20 MetLife Stadium	24 Soldier Field	28 Raymond James Stadium	32 University of Phoenix Stadium

The Uniforms

BRAND NAME

In 1919, the Indian Packing Company paid $500 for the team's uniforms and equipment. In exchange, the team was named for its first sponsor, and became the Packers.

Clay Matthews III was a later bloomer, as he was not even recruited to play college football. He eventually earned a spot at University of Southern California (USC) as a non-scholarship player.

An alumni of University of Notre Dame, Curly Lambeau selected navy blue and gold uniforms for his Green Bay Packers, so they might resemble his beloved alma mater. These uniforms gave rise to the nicknames "Blues" and "Big Bay Blues" given to the Packers in their early years. In 1950, the Packers changed their uniforms to hunter green and gold, another color scheme that contributed to the Packers' current nickname: "the Green and Gold."

Vince Lombardi again changed the uniforms in 1959. The bright green and gold lettering and the shiny green pants went in the wastebasket, and the Packers settled on the plainer color scheme of yellow, green, and white that remains to this day.

The Packers wore their throwback navy blue uniforms during the 2010 season.

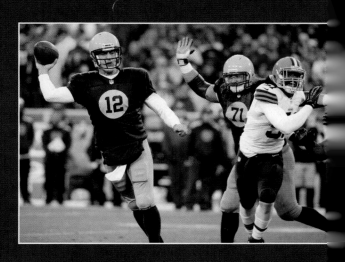

The Helmets

The Packers own the trademark for the "G" design. With permission from the team, the University of Georgia and Grambling State University have used a similar "G" design.

Some players wear a protective shield on their helmets that can help safeguard against a finger to the eye.

The Packers have had just one helmet **logo** in their long and storied history. While the sport of football has changed a great deal since 1961, the "G" embossed on the sides of the Green Bay Packers' helmets has not. Their logo looks the same today as it did the day it first appeared on the helmets of the soon-to-be world champions.

Before the "G" logo made its appearance, the Packers' helmets were altered a number of times. For the first 14 years of the franchise's existence, the helmets were brown leather. A yellow leather helmet, sometimes striped with green, replaced the brown ones from 1934 to 1950. In 1950, the NFL made the switch from leather to plastic helmets and the Packers chose gold. However, by 1954, the Packers wore yellow helmets, and in 1961, the "G" logo arrived to stay.

Grass on a football field can be slippery. NFL players wear shoes with cleats for better traction.

The Coaches

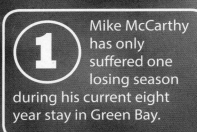

1 Mike McCarthy has only suffered one losing season during his current eight year stay in Green Bay.

With an 82-45 win-loss record, Mike McCarthy is not far from joining an exclusive club of Green Bay Packers' coaches who have won twice as many home games as they lost. This group includes Curly Lambeau, Vince Lombardi and Mike Holmgren.

Few coaches have influenced the culture of the NFL like Curly Lambeau and Vince Lombardi. The shadow cast by their legacies is indeed giant, but it gives Green Bay coaches the opportunity to prove themselves on football's most storied stage. Packers head coaches stand on the shoulders of giants. Those that rise to the occasion create legends of their own.

VINCE LOMBARDI

Vince Lombardi said, "Perfection is not attainable, but if we chase perfection we can catch excellence." In his hall of fame career, Lombardi's Packers won five NFL Championships in nine years. Lombardi holds the best playoff **winning percentage** of any coach in NFL history.

MIKE HOLMGREN

Mike Holmgren inherited a Packers team that had just two winning seasons in the previous 19 years. In seven years, Holmgren's Packers won three division titles and made the playoffs six straight times. Holmgren's quarterback coaching experience helped him to develop quarterback Brett Favre, whom he rode to victory in Super Bowl XXXI.

MIKE MCCARTHY

Mike McCarthy took the Pack to the **National Football Conference (NFC)** Championship Game in 2007, and then oversaw the rocky transition from Brett Favre to Aaron Rodgers. Favre went on to play for division rival Minnesota Vikings, while Rodgers developed into a league MVP and led the Pack to victory in Super Bowl XLV.

Team Spirit

AMERICA'S BiG CHEESE

The Packers have more fans on their waiting list for tickets (86,000) than actual seats in the stadium (72,928).

While the Packers do not think less of other teams for having mascots, they have never felt the need to carry on that tradition. Instead, the Packers have a tradition of dynamic and colorful personalities, both on the field and on the sidelines. From Curly Lambeau and Vince Lombardi to Brett Favre and Aaron Rodgers, the Packers have featured coaches that said memorable things off the field and players that performed memorable feats of heroism on it.

Packers fans are known as "Cheeseheads" because of the cheese production in the state of Wisconsin.

In addition to the long list of memorable players and coaches, Packers fans have always been a source of incredible passion and volume. Since 1999, the name "G-Force" has been used to describe the impact that Packers fans have on opposing players.

Each year, the team hosts a scrimmage called Family Night at Lambeau Field, regularly attracting more than 50,000 fans for this practice.

Legends of the Past

Many great players have suited up in the Packers' green and gold. A few of them have become icons of the team and the city it represents.

Bart Starr

Position Quarterback
Seasons 16 (1956–1971)
Born January 9, 1934, in Montgomery, Alabama

The quarterback that oversaw the first Packers revival was Bart Starr. A quiet child who lost his younger brother when he was only 13 years old, Starr was mostly overlooked during his time at the University of Alabama. However, an Alabama basketball coach recommended that the Packers take a close look at him. By 1960, Starr was participating in his first **Pro Bowl** as a representative of the Green Bay Packers. Starr went on to win five NFL Championships in seven years with the Packers. He was named MVP of Super Bowls I and II.

Reggie White

Between 1986 and 1998, Reggie White played in 13 straight Pro Bowls and recorded double-digits in **sacks** 11 times. Over that same span, he forced 33 fumbles and had more than 100 tackles in a season three times. Coming off of six-straight **All-Pro** seasons with the Philadelphia Eagles, White signed with the Packers in 1993. His presence transformed the Green Bay defense from a good one into a great one. Behind White, the 1996 Super Bowl Champion Packers allowed the fewest points in the NFL. In 1998, his last season in Green Bay, White was named NFL Defensive Player of the Year.

Position Defensive End
Seasons 15 (1984–2000)
Born December 19, 1961, in Chattanooga, Tennessee

Brett Favre

Brett Favre began a memorable run of three-straight NFL MVP awards in 1995. By the time he led the Packers to a Super Bowl championship in 1996, he was to the NFL what Michael Jordan was to the National Basketball Association. In 17 years with the Packers, Favre led the team to seven division titles and 11 playoff appearances. In 2007, his final season in Green Bay, he silenced the critics who had argued that he had hung on too long, registering a quarterback rating of 95.7, his highest since 1997. Favre was a remarkable athlete and fiery competitor who broke just about every passing record imaginable.

Position Quarterback
Seasons 20 (1991–2010)
Born October 10, 1969, in Gulfport, Mississippi

Charles Woodson

Coming out of the University of Michigan, pro scouts knew that Charles Woodson was a rare talent. In his senior season, Woodson played defensive end, returned kicks, and even saw some time as a wide receiver. To this day, he is the only defensive player to have won the **Heisman Trophy**.

In seven years with the Green Bay Packers, Woodson proved himself to be one of the league's toughest defensive backs. He battled back from injury to win the 2009 Defensive Player of the Year award and he became the only defensive player ever to make the Pro Bowl in three decades.

Position Defensive Back
Seasons 16 (1998–2013)
Born October 7, 1976, in Sebring, Ohio

Stars of Today

Today's Packers team is made up of many young, talented players who have proven that they are among the best players in the league.

Clay Matthews III

Clay Matthews began his college career as a walk-on at USC. While he excelled on special teams, he did not earn a starting position on the defense until his senior season. When Green Bay traded up to draft Matthews in the 2009 NFL Draft, many experts thought they were making a mistake. A four-time Pro Bowler, and the NFC's Defensive Player of the Year in 2010, Matthews has proven those experts wrong. Matthews is a member of a true football family. His grandfather, father, and uncle all played in the NFL, and his younger brother Casey plays linebacker for the Philadelphia Eagles.

Position Linebacker
Seasons 5 (2009–2013)
Born May 14, 1986, in Northridge, California

B. J. Raji

In 2010, 337-pound defensive tackle B.J. Raji became the dominant force in the middle that the Packers had hoped he would become. That season, Raji recorded 39 tackles, 6.5 sacks, and anchored a Green Bay defense that held numerous teams under 100 yards rushing en route to a Super Bowl title. During the Packers' 2010 playoff run, they began using Raji as a fullback in goal-line situations. As a result, Raji embraced the nickname "The Freezer," an homage to William "The Refrigerator" Perry, who was used similarly by the 1985 Chicago Bears.

Position Defensive Tackle
Seasons 5 (2009–2013)
Born July 11, 1986, in New York, New York

Jordy Nelson

In 2011, the Packers moved kick returner/wide receiver Jordy Nelson back to full-time receiver. They did not regret their decision. That season proved to be Nelson's breakout season, as he led the NFL's best offense with 68 receptions for 1,263 yards. His 15 receiving touchdowns were the third-highest single-season total in Packers' history. Nelson battled injuries in 2012, but kept up his high level of play. In 2013, despite an injury to Aaron Rodgers, Nelson again broke the 1,000-yard mark, cementing his reputation as a top-tier receiver.

Position Wide Receiver
Seasons 6 (2008–2013)
Born May 31, 1985, in Manhattan, Kansas

Aaron Rodgers

Aaron Rodgers currently holds the highest quarterback rating of all time. His incredible accuracy, high volume of touchdown passes, and low interception rates make him the greatest statistical quarterback the game has ever seen.

While Rodgers spent his first three years on Green Bay's bench, he did not complain. Instead, he learned all he could from Brett Favre and waited patiently for his moment in the sun. Few were prepared for how brightly he would shine. A three-time Pro Bowler, Rodgers was named the MVP of Super Bowl XLV and NFL MVP in 2011.

Position Quarterback
Seasons 9 (2005–2013)
Born December 2, 1983, in Chico, California

All-Time Records

112   Single-season Receptions

Sterling Sharpe was at the top of his game in 1993 when he caught 112 passes for 1,274 yards.

8,322   Career Rushing Yards

Ahman Green was virtually unstoppable in the early- to mid-2000s. In 2003, he set the franchise's single-season rushing record with 1,883 yards.

45
Single-season Touchdown Passes

In Aaron Rodgers' remarkable 2011 MVP season, he set a Green Bay record for touchdown passes and only threw six interceptions.

61,655
All-time Passing Yards

Brett Favre is the only quarterback in NFL history to throw for more than 70,000 passing yards. More than 60,000 of those came with the Green Bay Packers.

10,137
Career Receiving Yards

In 14 outstanding seasons with the Pack, Donald Driver topped gifted receivers such as Sterling Sharpe and James Lofton in career receiving yards.

Timeline

Throughout the team's history, the Green Bay Packers have had many memorable events that have become defining moments for the team and its fans.

August 11, 1919
Curly Lambeau and George Whitney Calhoun found the Green Bay Packers.

1961
One season after their first playoff appearance since 1945, the Pack win their second-straight division title and advance to the NFL Championship Game. Behind the play of NFL MVP Paul Hornung, Bart Starr, and Ron Kramer, they annihilate the NY Giants, 37-0.

January 15, 1967
The Packers play in the first-ever Super Bowl, a championship game between the winners of the **American Football League (AFL)** and the NFL. Bart Starr earns Super Bowl MVP honors, as the Packers destroy the Kansas City Chiefs, 35-10.

| 1905 | 1920 | 1935 | 1950 | 1965 | 1980 |

1929
The Packers' defense allows just 22 points in the entire 13-game season, an average of 1.7 points per game. They finish with the league's best record and win the first of three consecutive NFL titles.

In 1965, following a two-year absence, the Pack make it back to the playoffs behind the play of NFL MVP Bart Starr and the league's best defense.

February 2, 1959
The Packers hire new head coach Vince Lombardi. Lombardi's impact on the team is immediate, as he transforms them from a 1-10 laughing stock into a 7-5 contender in a single season.

The Future
Aaron Rodgers is an MVP who leads by example and excels under pressure. As long as he's on the field, he will utilize weapons like Jordy Nelson and Eddie Lacy to light up scoreboards. If the Packers want to earn a trip back to the Super Bowl, it will be up to the Packers' defense to match the play of their high-scoring offense.

January 26, 1997
Following a dominant season in which the Packers win 13 games for the second time in franchise history, Brett Favre and Super Bowl MVP Desmond Howard lead the Packers to a victory over the New England Patriots in Super Bowl XXXI.

In 2011, Aaron Rodgers registers the greatest statistical season in the history of the NFL and is named league MVP.

| 1990 | 1995 | 2000 | 2005 | 2010 | 2015 |

In 2007, under second-year coach Mike McCarthy, Favre ends a three-year Pro Bowl absence and leads the Pack to another division title.

1993
After only two playoff appearances in 26 years, a Packers revival is sparked by head coach Mike Holmgren, third-year quarterback Brett Favre, and offseason acquisition Reggie White. The Packers beat the Detroit Lions in the wild card round behind Favre's three touchdown passes to Sterling Sharpe.

February 6, 2011
After sneaking into the playoffs, the Packers advance to the Super Bowl for the first time in 13 years. Aaron Rodgers throws for 304 yards and three touchdowns and the Packers beat the Pittsburgh Steelers, 31-25 in the first Super Bowl match-up between two perennial champions.

Write a Biography

Life Story

A person's life story can be the subject of a book. This kind of book is called a biography. Biographies often describe the lives of people who have achieved great success. These people may be alive today, or they may have lived many years ago. Reading a biography can help you learn more about a great person.

Get the Facts

Use this book, and research in the library and on the Internet, to find out more about your favorite Packer. Learn as much about this player as you can. What position does he play? What are his statistics in important categories? Has he set any records? Also, be sure to write down key events in the person's life. What was his childhood like? What has he accomplished off the field? Is there anything else that makes this person special or unusual?

Use the Concept Web

A concept web is a useful research tool. Read the questions in the concept web on the following page. Answer the questions in your notebook. Your answers will help you write a biography.

Concept Web

Adulthood
- Where does this individual currently reside?
- Does he or she have a family?

Your Opinion
- What did you learn from the books you read in your research?
- Would you suggest these books to others?
- Was anything missing from these books?

Childhood
- Where and when was this person born?
- Describe his or her parents, siblings, and friends.
- Did this person grow up in unusual circumstances?

Accomplishments off the Field
- What is this person's life's work?
- Has he or she received awards or recognition for accomplishments?
- How have this person's accomplishments served others?

Write a Biography

Help and Obstacles
- Did this individual have a positive attitude?
- Did he or she receive help from others?
- Did this person have a mentor?
- Did this person face any hardships?
- If so, how were the hardships overcome?

Accomplishments on the Field
- What records does this person hold?
- What key games and plays have defined his or her career?
- What are his or her stats in categories important to his or her position?

Work and Preparation
- What was this person's education?
- What was his or her work experience?
- How does this person work; what is the process he or she uses?

Trivia Time

Take this quiz to test your knowledge of the Green Bay Packers.
The answers are printed upside-down under each question.

1 Who quarterbacked the Green Bay Packers to five NFL Championships in seven years?

A. Bart Starr

2 Which former Packers head coach is their home stadium named for?

A. Curly Lambeau

3 Which Packers player was named NFL Defensive Player of the Year in 1998?

A. Reggie White

4 Which Green Bay Packer is nicknamed "The Freezer?"

A. B.J. Raji

5 How many NFL and Super Bowl championships have the Packers won in their history?

A. 13

6 In what year did the "G" logo on the Packers' helmet first appear?

A. 1961

7 Which former Packers coach has the best playoff winning percentage of any coach in NFL history?

A. Vince Lombardi

8 Which current Packers player has a younger brother that plays for the Philadelphia Eagles?

A. Clay Matthews III

9 Which Packers quarterback won three-straight NFL MVP awards?

A. Brett Favre

10 How many Packers have been inducted into the NFL Hall of Fame?

A. 22

Key Words

American Football League (AFL): a major American Professional Football league that operated from 1960 until 1969, when it merged with the National Football League (NFL)

All-Pro: an NFL player judged to be the best in his position for a given season

hall of fame: a group of persons judged to be outstanding in a particular sport

Heisman Trophy: an annual award given to the college football player who best demonstrates excellence and hard work

logo: a symbol that stands for a team or organization

most valuable player (MVP): the player judged to be most valuable to his team's success

NFL Draft: an annual event where the NFL chooses college football players to be new team members

playoffs: the games played following the end of the regular season. Six teams are qualified: the four winners of the different conferences, and the two best teams that did not finish first in their respective conference (the wild cards)

postseason: a sporting event that takes place after the end of the regular season

Pro Bowl: the annual all-star game for NFL players pitting the best players in the National Football Conference against the best players in the American Football Conference

sacks: a sack occurs when the quarterback is tackled behind the line of scrimmage before he can throw a forward pass

Super Bowl: the NFL's annual championship game between the winning team from the NFC and the winning team from the AFC

winning percentage: the number of games won divided by the total number of games played; a coach with 7 wins in 10 games would have a winning percentage of 70 percent

Index

Log on to www.av2books.com

AV² by Weigl brings you media enhanced books that support active learning. Go to www.av2books.com, and enter the special code found on page 2 of this book. You will gain access to enriched and enhanced content that supplements and complements this book. Content includes video, audio, weblinks, quizzes, a slide show, and activities.

AV² Online Navigation

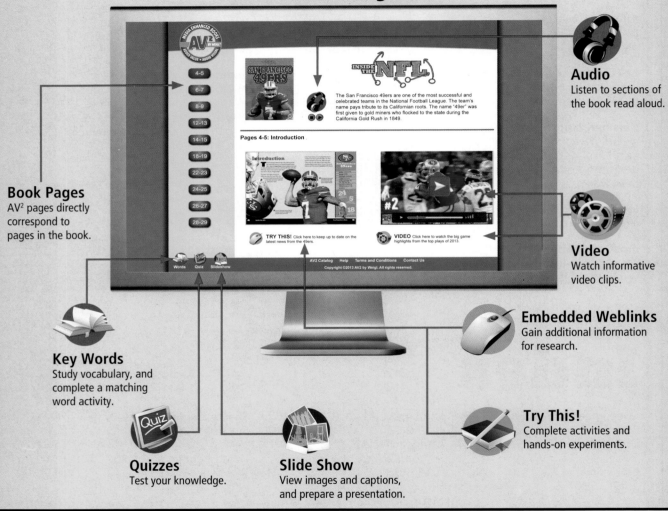

Audio
Listen to sections of the book read aloud.

Book Pages
AV² pages directly correspond to pages in the book.

Video
Watch informative video clips.

Key Words
Study vocabulary, and complete a matching word activity.

Embedded Weblinks
Gain additional information for research.

Quizzes
Test your knowledge.

Slide Show
View images and captions, and prepare a presentation.

Try This!
Complete activities and hands-on experiments.

AV² was built to bridge the gap between print and digital. We encourage you to tell us what you like and what you want to see in the future.

Sign up to be an AV² Ambassador at www.av2books.com/ambassador.